AF504713

Why Women Stay When They Want to Go

Why Women Stay When They Want to Go

by Jeannie Middleton

Charleston, SC
www.PalmettoPublishing.com

Why Women Stay When They Want to Go

Copyright © 2022 by Jeannie Middleton

All rights reserved.

No portion of this book may be reproduced, stored in a retrieval system, or transmitted in any form by any means—electronic, mechanical, photocopy, recording, or other—except for brief quotations in printed reviews, without prior permission of the author.

First Edition

Hardcover ISBN: 979-8-88590-935-8
Paperback ISBN: 979-8-88590-936-5
eBook ISBN: 979-8-88590-937-2

Dedicated to My Sister
Jayne Dietl

In Loving Memory of
My Sister Marriane Greco

$\mathcal{I}$ remember spending my teenage years hanging out with many friends. We found our first loves, went to dance clubs, and some-times hung out in the park talking about what we hoped our futures would be. We imagined the type of men we would marry and we all shared the same dream of a big house, a white picket fence, several children, and a good husband. None of us had come from money; we all had our first jobs by the age of fifteen. We learned that if we wanted something, we either had to work for it or use hand-me-downs.

My friend Sarah was a very determined girl. She always knew exactly what she wanted. If Sarah saw a blouse in the store window, she would wait until payday and buy it. If Sarah saw a guy that she was attracted to, she stopped at nothing until she got him to take her out on a date—but then again, it wasn't that much of a struggle for Sarah. She was a popular girl in town. Those teenage years were full of fun, with lots of laughs and parties, but they went by fast. It seemed we went from riding bikes and living at home under our parents' thumbs to driving cars and living in our own apartments within the blink of an eye.

Some of my friends went off to college and others ended up marrying young. Sarah was one of those friends that got married too young. She became pregnant. Back in the day, you didn't get pregnant unless you were already married—she ended up doing the opposite by marrying after pregnancy. Although she had a lot of support throughout her pregnancy and her marriage, things didn't work out too well for her. She found herself home all of the time, having to tend to her newborn son while her husband went out straight from work. Sometimes he wouldn't come home, leaving Sarah alone to feel unhappy and unloved. Her marriage was nowhere, yet Sarah stayed, hoping things would change. Unfortunately, they didn't. Their marriage got worse every day. Sarah became depressed. I remember shaking my head and thinking wow, Sarah was such a go-getter, such a strong and determined woman, who was never afraid to speak up. It was hard for me to imagine why Sarah would stay in a marriage that was so toxic; it really puzzled me. When I asked Sarah about the issue, she replied with, "Where will I go? Who will want me with a child? I don't want to be alone."

Sarah claimed she was scared to stand on her own. I pointed out that she was standing on her own because her husband was never there. I tried to help her see that she could make it without him. It would be difficult. Sarah and I spoke for hours, day in, day out, until years later, things clicked and Sarah got a part-time job, a babysitter. She started to go out and socialize, but I noticed that she would cling to the first male that paid attention to her—my red flag went up! I tried to warn Sarah to slow down, but she saw an opportunity to feel needed and loved, and was blinded by the fact that another man was willing to have her and her son.

There was no stopping her.

John showered her with dinners, dancing out on the town, vacations. She saw that as love. I saw it as lust and control—but at this point, there was no getting through to her. She went through with her divorce only to marry again. John was a man with a good job that wanted to buy a house and give Sarah everything—it all came with a price. He told Sarah she had to separate herself from me; he was all she would need. I told her that he saw me as a threat because we're so close. He was afraid Sarah would love me more than him. Without me in the picture all the attention.

Sarah loved the gifts, jewelry, vacations, having a house to call her home—things appeared great for her and we grew further and further apart. She even had two more children and we seldom spoke. It was heartbreaking to lose the close bond that was developed over many years, but John wanted it that way. Sarah began to settle down with her new life.

Years later, my phone rang. I answered it only to hear Sarah's voice whispering through the phone, speaking carefully so that John wouldn't hear. She called me several times this way, speaking softly, then rushing off the phone, saying, "I have to hang up. John is coming." I strongly sensed that something was wrong, but Sarah would only tell me how wonderful things were. I was confused, until one day I ran into her at a grocery store. We talked for a few minutes. Her cellphone rang. John calling. I could hear him yelling through the phone, saying things like, "Where the hell are you?" and "What's taking you so long?" Then I heard him accusing her of having an affair with a cashier at the supermarket. Sarah was embarrassed but made light of the situation. I interpreted it as a serious problem within her marriage and felt that maybe one day she would reach her limit and let me in on what was going on between them. In the meantime, I started to engage with my other childhood friends to see how they were doing with their relationships.

I made lunch plans with Bella. To my surprise, she had no problem opening up to me. She was telling me she was trapped in a marriage that had gone sour a year after they said their vows. Bella openly admitted that her husband would hit her if dinner wasn't served by a certain time, or if his clothes had a wrinkle in them. I asked Bella, "Why don't you leave him?" But she was committed to staying because getting a divorce was a sin in the eyes of God.

"You think God wants you to be unhappy and get beat up all the time?" I argued. "You're willing to stay in an abusive marriage because you think it's a sin to get a divorce? Bella, it's a sin that your husband beats you. You're not a punching bag; God loves you and if you reach out to God and pray on it, I promise you, God will set you free."

Two years later, I found out that Bella's husband was killed in a horrific car crash. Sad to admit, but when that happened, she felt like the weight on her shoulders was lifted. We got together after the funeral and she said to me, "I'm scared to love again." Bella got so used to being abused by her husband that unless there was conflict. Fortunately, she sought counseling, which helped her learn to love herself and regain her self-worth. Bella went on to college and became a counselor. She is finally out of the woods and happy for the first time in years.

My other childhood friend Patricia also had a story to tell. Her husband, Sam, was having an affair with another woman, and Patricia was well aware of it. They both slept in separate bedrooms, and Patricia chose to put blindfolds on. She was depressed and used food to suppress her unhappiness, which caused her to gain weight, bringing her total weight to 310 pounds. So here you have a beautiful woman, struggling with her weight, unhappy, and eats to survive her sadness. She's a great mom, who loves her children, but she didn't realize that she was teaching her children that it was okay to be unhappy and unloved.

I spent time talking to Patricia, pointing out. I told her to value herself, love herself, and give herself permission to be happy. I encouraged her to go on a diet and join a gym so she could be healthy. I said, "Patricia, stop making excuses, stop believing that you don't deserve better." Patricia needed to hear this, and she pushed forward. She changed her diet and began taking walks every day with her children. After six months of hard work, she lost seventy pounds. Once Patricia saw the results, she didn't want to stop. She started to like what she saw and slowly found her new self, gaining confidence, and became mentally strong.

After two long years, Patricia was down to 145 pounds.

Patricia was on fire with new dreams for her new self and her children. She thanked me for helping her get to where she should be, then she threw her husband out of the house and tossed his clothes to the front lawn, closing the door behind him. Sam was devastated and stood there in disbelief. He told her he was sorry and wanted to start over, but Patricia wasn't making any more excuses; she wanted him out and a divorce. She could finally live, so she took all her excuses of being overweight and undeserving of love, and all the reasons why she felt she didn't deserve to be happy and wrote them down on a piece of paper to bury them deep in the ground. Since her divorce, she learned how to spend time on herself, pampering herself, and enjoys the space she gets. Now she goes on vacations with her children, coaches her daughters' basketball team, and is finally happy.

I am happy Patricia was able to escape her bad marriage and find happiness, so I guess it's time to revisit Sarah. It's been two years since I had seen Sarah. We spoke on the phone from time to time but it was just not the same as going to lunch together. Instead of going out, Sarah invited me over to her house for lunch, which I found odd. Something was up. When I got there, Sarah opened up to me for the first time, but only because her husband was on a trip with his friends. Sarah finally had enough privacy to speak, and I came to find that Sarah's life was worse than I could have imagined. John was so controlling that she wasn't living her life; she was merely existing.

She wasn't allowed to go anywhere or have friends. Her husband constantly put her down so she didn't have an ounce of confidence or self-esteem. To me, John was worse than the devil himself. He not only controlled her, but he abused all three of her children. The whole family had to walk on eggshells around him. He controlled everywhere Sarah went, obsessively checking her phone, accusing her of "screwing around" behind his back, especially if she took too long at the grocery store. Sarah said early on in the relationship that his jealousy was flattering to her; she thought it symbolized how much he loved her. It took about twenty-five years for her to realize that jealousy did not mean love—it's a sickness. By the time Sarah realized it was abuse, she was so used to that lifestyle that it became normal to her. Changing that lifestyle was very frightening and felt nearly impossible. John governed so much of her life that she hardly had a life of her own. She could barely even laugh without John ridiculing her for laughing, screaming at her, "What's so funny? Why are you laughing?" Then he would accuse her of laughing at him. Sarah would say that she'd never be free until the day he died. I told her that's not true and that she has a choice; she could leave with her three children and stay with a friend or go to a shelter. If she left, he would find her and kill her. There was no way to throw him out of the house without him attacking her, so her only choice was to remain unhappy and pray he dies. "Wow!" I said. "Sarah, look at you; look at your life. You're so broken down."

She agreed and said, "Yes, I am like a broken toy and no one wants to play with a broken toy." My heart went out to her, and I tried so hard to tell her that this was no way to live—she had to get away and start over, but her fears overcame anything I said.

Ten more unhappy years went by, and Sarah was still in the same boat that continued to sink with no life preserves available. She was still being abused both verbally and physically, and she was in worse condition than she had ever been before. Sarah tried to commit suicide—anything to get away from her husband—her health deteriorated, and she needed to go to the hospital for surgery. She prayed that something, anything would go wrong so she could stay in the hospital, and I encouraged her not to wish for such things. I said, "Please be careful what you wish for." It wasn't a surprise to me, but as faith would have it, the surgery did not go well, and Sarah got what she wished for. Sarah was transferred to another hospital for more surgeries, which turned into a stay that lasted over a month. She was overjoyed that she didn't have to go home and deal with John's abuse, but the abuse didn't stop, and John decided to stay every day at the hospital with her. It was like a living hell. If a doctor came in to examine Sarah, John would make horrible comments to her such as, "You let him touch you. I know you liked it."

Sarah broke down and sank further into depression. Months went by and I would visit her at the hospital, and John would try to keep me away. He controlled who got to visit with her, leaving her with no say. After about a four-month long hospital stay, Sarah finally went home only to face her demon and go back to the lifestyle she left behind. Another ten years came and went, but this time, John's mental state started to change. He became forgetful and even more abusive than before. He became violent. Sarah felt that all his years of drinking were finally taking a toll on him, but it was more than that— John's mental state was not the only thing changing. His physical health was changing too. John got an infection in his foot, which led to several hospital stays, each lasting several weeks at a time. Sarah was forced to stay in a chair in the hospital room each and every time. Things got so bad with John's health that he had to have his foot amputated. You'd think that Sarah would start to find some joy in her life knowing that John was now hindered by a wheelchair, maybe now she would be able to find more freedom and room to breathe, but that definitely wasn't the case. Every second, John needed her assistance. I remember her saying she hoped he would be placed in a nursing home because she couldn't handle the way things were. She would say, "I can't do this. I don't want to do this. I am done. I am cooked, fried like a turkey." Sarah was at her limit. She spent forty years being abused and tortured both mentally and physically.

John did end up back in the hospital, but this time, they had to remove half of his leg. I remember going there to support Sarah. Even I dealt with John's abuse that day. He yelled at me to get the hell out, leave, and I simply ignored him. He couldn't get up and run after me, so I stayed and gave Sarah a break. I told her to go outside and get some fresh air and coffee. I noticed once Sarah saw she had support and was able to take a break from John, she visibly calmed down. Meanwhile, John screamed the whole time while she was away, "Sarah! Where the hell are you?" over and over again. The doctors, nurses, and staff were fed up, yet John refused to stop yelling. Once Sarah came back, I told her that I have been around sick people and I can tell when they're getting ready to pass away. I said, "Sarah, John is dying." She laughed it off and didn't believe it, but I told her that I'd seen what death looks like. He had a grey tint to his face. Even then she couldn't see what I saw, so she wasn't prepared for the following day. John was transferred to a nursing home and approximately twenty hours after being there, Sarah received a phone call telling her that John passed away. Sarah called me and told me the news. I went there and stayed with her, sitting beside John's bed as we said our goodbyes. We waited for the children to come and say their goodbyes, then we went to Sarah's house to make the funeral arrangements. I waited until after the funeral to have a conversation with her because I knew the hardest part for Sarah was only beginning. Years of not being allowed to talk freely on the phone or go for errands without someone calling and questioning where she was, whom she was with, and when she'd be back had an impact. She didn't know what to do or how to move forward. She was always scared, waiting for her phone to ring and for that voice to yell at her.

"Wow," Sarah said, "I lived in so much fear waiting for the bomb to drop." I told her it's okay to feel that way, but she didn't have to live in fear anymore or worry about checking over her shoulder. No one would hurt her anymore; her forty years of hell were over. It took John's death for her to find some type of self-esteem, moments to smile and laugh. A good two years to finally stop feeling guilty about laughing, smiling, and saying whatever came to her mind. She even stopped checking over her shoulder. Now I look at Sarah and see a beautiful rose blooming. I know Sarah still has a long way to go but it's a new beginning for her. With each new day that goes by, I watch Sarah grow and get stronger. I watch her grasp her independence, her freedom of speech. Her life begins to unfold. Sarah and I even take short vacations together. We have fun and laughs, now we say "the boogie man" can't hurt her anymore; he is gone forever. Now the sun can shine and wash away the rain.

I know Sarah will be okay; she learned to live, to breathe, and to exist.

I ask why do women stay when they should go. Some women feel trapped and see no way out, so they stay unhappy in a toxic relationship. Other women feel that if they are not in an abusive relationship, they are not loved. In that case, I believe it's because some women grow up in toxic homes where they learn that it's okay to be abused. They deal with abusive, toxic, alcoholic parents, and they recognize that as the only lifestyle they know, so when they're older, they look for abusive men. It makes them feel loved. Without the abuse, they feel empty as though something in their life is missing. Other women stay because they're too afraid to live on their own. They may have had a parent who was domineering and controlling and told them that they are a nobody and will never amount to anything in life, and no one will ever love them. Some parents themselves are very cold and un-emotional, so that's the only way they know how to treat their kids. No one knows any better, and this learned behavior of being cold and unemo-tional continues to be taught. The children they raise are starved for love and attention, so the children grow up feeling something is missing but can't quite put their finger on what is actually missing because they never had the love and at-tention they should have gotten. Everything goes from one generation to another generation. Some would say, in the DNA.

Now, let's take my friends Julie and Anna. Julie was raised in a tight-knit family, loved by both of her parents, who provided a stable home. Her dad had a good job and her mom cooked, cleaned, and took care of the household chores. Julie's brother played sports and the whole family went together to support him at his games. Julie's family was so loving she never had to question whether she was loved or not. When she fell in love, married her childhood sweetheart, they both supported each other in a healthy way. They shared the duties of caring for their home and children equally. Their marriage.

Now if we look at Anna's life growing up, her parents fought a lot, almost every day. They would scream at each other—you couldn't get her parents to agree on anything. Anna withdrew from everyone; she was a loner and liked being by herself. She wouldn't dare have a friend come over because she was too embarrassed. Her life could have gone in any direction, good or bad, but she was determined to be nothing like her parents. Instead, Anna chose to become a social worker, not only to help others but also to understand people and their behavior. Anna followed her dreams and became a very successful social worker. Anna shared a story with me about her friend Margie. She could never understand why Margie married a man who was just like her father. Margie's dad was a drunk. There wasn't a day that went by where he didn't drink. When he walked through the door, he was verbally abusive and told Margie that she would never amount to anything and that she wasn't worth anything. Margie grew to hate herself and was made to feel like she didn't deserve anything good in life. She became a punching bag for all the men she came in contact with. Each of her relationships was with a heavy drinker that abused her both physically and verbally. All of them walked out on her, leaving Margie hurt, beaten down, alone, and depressed. Her depression became so bad that she voluntarily went into a hospital for mental help. It's good that she recognized that she needed help and sought it, but she met someone in the mental facility that was being treated for alcoholism and she chose to cling to him. Harry drank so much that he had developed cirrhosis. He was not healthy, but he couldn't stop drinking. Margie and Harry got together after leaving the program. He moved into Margie's apartment. After two years, they got married. While Margie worked at a diner as a waitress, Harry stayed home and didn't contribute anything to the high cost of living. He let all the expenses fall on Margie and she let this happen because she didn't believe that she would ever amount to anything. She thought she better keep working and paying the bills because if she didn't, Harry would leave her and she would end up alone again. She accepted Harry and his drinking habit because that's what she grew up with. Margie learned to take care of her dad; it was her responsibility to cook, clean, and take care of the laundry. She never really had a childhood. She missed the simple joys of learning to ride a bike and instead had to focus on bigger responsibilities.

Her life growing up was very much the same as her married life. It all seemed normal to her until one day, shortly after Harry passed away from alcohol poisoning and cirrhosis, Margie decided to join a group for dealing with the loss of a loved one. Joining that group turned out to be the best thing Margie ever did. Not only did she make new friends, she also learned so much about herself. Aside from learning to cope with the loss of her dad and Harry, she learned that marriage is a shared responsibility and it's okay to let someone love you. Margie was told "She is somebody, and learned about learned behaviors," positive thoughts, and most of all, she learned that she wasn't on this earth to be walked all over or treated as someone's punching bag. She learned to accept appreciation and acknowledgement for all the good things she did. Now she is a new woman with a good handle on things. It took five years of hard work and friends that didn't give up on her, but it was all worth it. Margie met someone and is happy for the first time in her life. Now she gets taken out to dinners, movies. Life is good for her.

Life, as you can see, can be a vicious cycle when you stay in a relationship that your heart wants out of. Look deep within yourself and ask yourself questions. Start with, how was your upbringing; were your parents loving, supportive, and compassionate? Were there problems? Be honest with yourself, meditate, and take the time to create the life you really want. The truth is there is nothing you can't do if you put your mind to it. You can change things, but only if you take a good look in the mirror and make the decision to love yourself. It's all up to you. But what I am seeing is too many women choosing to stay in an unhappy, unhealthy, or abusive relationship. It's time for women to allow themselves to be loved, to feel worth it, and to know they deserve to be loved. Women, I speak to all of you: put away your boxing gloves, throw them in the trash—it's time to stop beating yourself up. Stop punishing yourself, you're not that little girl anymore and any demons you may have had in your past are gone forever if you let them go. Take all the hurt, the pain, the harsh words, the beatings, and put them in a big black trash bag and place it in a trash can with the lid shut tight. Watch as the garbage men empty the trash and know that all the hurt, the pain, the beatings, the harsh words someone may have said to you are now gone; they are never coming back. Then take a deep breath and enjoy the fresh air. Your fresh start in life is about to begin; feel the weight of the world lift off your shoulders, and take your first steps. It'll seem like you're learning to walk for the first time. Before you know it, you'll be running. Run with life, joy, love, and laughter— you deserve it all, and it's yours for the taking. It awaits you, and you just have to want it.

Get out in the world, dream on, dream big, climb those stairs to the top, and don't look back. Put on a pretty dress, slip your feet into those heels you bought but never wore, then dance. While you're dancing, see and feel the woman you have become.

When I was young, I saw so much as a child—so many different personalities; there was drama, separations, gains, and losses. I saw rich people, poor people, happiness, and sadness. I saw pain in so many people. I remember this young couple who had a four-year-old son. They lived on the water. One day, their little boy walked out on the deck and fell into the water and drowned. Everyone was touched by the death of such a young, beautiful boy. There wasn't a dry eye at the funeral, but there beside the little casket was a poem that I wrote for the parents because I felt the pain that they could not speak of.

KEVIN

On the very day God decided to take Kevin away,

A vision of happiness he was to his Mother's eyes

As she prayed beside him,

Then said goodbye.

Aunts, uncles, neighbors and friends

Gathered around to see someone so dear,

That was loved by everyone,

Who died this past year.

The beautiful Mother of Kevin

Stood beside him

Looking so stunned,

Trying to say what she really fels,

But that choked up feeling,

Just won't disappear.

Part of my childhood years involved seeing my friends falling in and out of love, and watching some turn to drugs. This prompted me to write another poem called "Life."

LIFE

Life right here in front of you,

Watching everything you do,

Giving you peace and happiness, and other
things if you seldom ask of it,

Life is a ride,

A sweet hello and a kiss goodbye,

A path to follow,

In which some don't,

With time to turn back,

But some just won't,

Life is a road that leads to torture or fun,

To debts of bills, taking drugs, popping pills,

Life is a laugh,

When you learn of the things you did in the past,

The mistakes you made much too fast,

The shadows you saw in the darkness of night,

The running you did when times weren't right,

Your first love, and how it was found,

You with your false eyelashes and make-
believe nails,

And him, the apple of your eye,

A kiss on the cheek,

A pull on your blouse,

Hoping to get a peek,

All of this is Life,

And we must face it.

When we get older,

Our thoughts all change,

But our memories still remain,

This is Life and what it's about,

Beyond the tears and loneliness,

This is Life,

The wandering of the break of day,

If you're still around

Come time to pray,

All of this is Life,

And Life goes on

Even after we are gone.

I had another friend of mine who went to work each day, made dinner for her husband and children, took care of the laundry, cleaned the house, and still made time to have an extra-marital affair. She did this because she was unhappy. She never felt appreciated for anything she did. Her husband took her for granted, and she stayed in the marriage when she wanted to go. I wrote another poem because I felt her every emotion, pain, and her loneliness. I just wished she was strong enough to take the bull by the horns. Instead, she stayed when she wanted to go; she stayed out of convenience. I guess you could say she had the best of both worlds.

THOUGHTS OF YOU AND I

Thoughts of you and I

Somehow passed us by,

Dreams of yesterday in blue skies

Are now nightmares,

I can't seem to hide,

The fun and games

That we would play,

Like everything else,

Went away,

The love, passion, warmth, and joy

That once brought us together

Came back again,

But this time to destroy,

Thoughts are no longer of you and I,

But of someone else

I'll forever hold inside,

Dreams can no longer come true,

It's hard to dream of one

And live with another.

Too many women stay in a relationship when they want to go. It's a choice they make because they feel stuck, scared, or guilty for even thinking about leaving. Women need to value themselves. I tell women it's okay to be happy, give yourself permission. It's okay to fall short of God's glory. God will lift you up. It's okay to make mistakes and learn from them, but it's not okay to just survive and go through the motions to be unhappy or taken advantage of. No, it's downright not acceptable; it's time women take a stand, find their place in life and go live it to the fullest because there are no second chances—life will end.

Women need to be taught that they are put on this earth to have children, cook, clean, and please a man. Women should have choices. If a woman wants to do a man's job, she should be able to make that choice. Women can do it. . . . If a woman chooses to have children, but it's got to be something they want to do. I don't believe that any woman out there chooses to be abused by a boyfriend, husband, father, etc. I believe the woman may not have noticed the signs early on, and that later when the abuse starts, maybe the woman hoped it would change. The truth is it doesn't change and the signs are there; what's in the beginning will be there till the end. Women need to stand their ground and plant both feet. Open your eyes; when you see the first sign of abuse, pull out your stop sign and put the abuse to an end. Don't let fear, threats, guilt, low confidence, or any of that stand in the way.

A woman told me that they put up with so much abuse because their partner threatened to kill their whole family. It's true that several men have said those words to women and a woman's response is, "Okay, I will do whatever it takes to keep my family alive, even if it means being verbally abused, raped, and beaten." The women fall right into what I call the Bully Trap: a trap, until they can't take it anymore and become so broken that they just lie down and die. Sounds harsh but no truer words have been spoken.

After years of abuse, the woman grabbed her family and left town only to be found again by the man they were running from. The bully who shook this woman's life to a point where she wanted to die gave up when he realized that he couldn't get to her anymore or scare her with his threats. This time, when he found her, she didn't run. She didn't even respond to him or his threats, so he moved on to abuse other women instead. As for her, she realized years later that her family was safe and she became angry at herself for allowing him to have the control over her to live in a state of fear, but she had lost years of her life. She truly believed he would kill her children, her whole family, so she was willing to surrender to him to save them. She didn't realize that along the way, she stopped living and brought her family down with her. She couldn't take her kids to the park or the beach because he wouldn't let her go anywhere. She couldn't tell anyone what was going on because she feared he would kill them all. So, women, wake up if this should ever happen to you or is happening, remember that 99 percent of such threats are only scare tactics, and nothing more. To all women, who need to hear this, stand tall; take your place in life; let no man ever threaten you with scare tactics, and don't let yourself become another victim. It's only words, and words can't hurt you! Remember that these things are going on but they don't have to continue. Don't live in fear—don't do it to yourself or your family. There is help out there, please reach out and grab it. Don't stay when you want to go.

I spoke with an old friend whom I hadn't seen in years. I saw that she was always with her and that she looked happy. Her boyfriend was a much older man. I used to say to myself, maybe that's the answer—an older man. But truth be told, that was far from reality. I would never have guessed it at all; her boyfriend had a gun and when he got home, he would hold that gun to her head and threaten to pull the trigger. She began to hide in the closet when she knew he was on his way home. She was another woman scared to tell anyone about her situation for the fear that he would kill her and her children. She started staying at a friend's house because she was too scared to go home. She later learned that her boyfriend could have pulled the trigger—he served fourteen years in prison for killing his own mother. He stabbed his mother twenty-one times and watched her take her last breath. When she found out, he was history; she left with her two children, but do you see what it took? Can you imagine bearing two children with a murderer and not knowing? This woman survived having a gun held to her head, living in fear; she's lucky to be alive to share her story. He later died a slow death. This time the tables were turned. She was there to watch him take his last breath. He died of Lou Gehrig's disease. She stood there and said to him as he took his last breath, "You tried to destroy me, my life, my will to live, but I am still here, and I will survive and learn to live again. Take my fear and all those bad memories with you." It's hard to believe that she had no idea whom she was living with but it's all true. There's so much going on in people's lives, but most are too afraid to tell anyone and they stay for so long because of fear.

Fear is an ugly word. It is sad that this type of bullying goes on every day. It truly has to stop. There must be a way to educate women prior to entering any relationship; a safe place should be available for these women, a hot line. The system must change. These bullies must pay for all the lives they've destroyed; there must be consequences. The men that hurt and destroy women's lives go unpunished for way too long so help me get the word out there, and maybe more women will come forward and be spared. Let's stand together as one. I say to all women out there if you're reading this book and you are one of these women being abused, put your abuser's name out there, I promise you he will go into hiding.

IF

If only I saw the signs early on,

I would not have been abused,

If only I wasn't so afraid,

I wouldn't have stayed,

If only there was help,

I could have escaped.

There's hope and help for the poor,

Only pain and suffering for one whose been
clawed,

There's hope and help for the hungry,

It's called food stamps,

There's hope and help for the sick,

It's called Medicaid,

But where's the help for the abused?

Where do they go?

And the abuser, what price do they pay?

If only there was a place,

I could feel safe,

I wouldn't have stayed.

We see the many reasons why women stay when they want to go. Just the other day, I ran into a longtime friend. She's with someone she said is such a nice guy but there's no chemistry. She doesn't want to use him or take advantage of him, so she's honest with him. But he tries to convince her to try to make it work. I think he doesn't want to be alone. That, in my opinion, is choosing a road that leads to nowhere, just a dead end. Being in a relationship solely because you don't want to be alone is definitely not a good idea. There must be some chemistry and trust. I know things happen in life. Sometimes our partners pass away or become ill and can't take care of themselves. We have to start over and maybe find another relationship, but remember what you see in the beginning of any relationship is what you'll see in the end. Many women tend to think that they can change the flaws they find in their man, but it's not true—we can't change them; we can only change ourselves. There are brilliant women out there who have had unplanned pregnancies, but they have made good choices. They've had their children and raised them on their own, relying on themselves as they worked and climbed the ladder of success. They are single parents that deserve a lot of credit—because they never gave up. They worked hard and made good lives for themselves. They don't manipulate the father of their child to get married because they knew a relationship like that wouldn't work out. There are women that deliberately get pregnant, thinking that their man will be forced to stay with them, but that's not always true. Making a relationship like that work is like finding a needle in a haystack. Relationships mean work. When you have a good relationship for a long time, you'll find there's less to talk about. The key is to know this and find ways to wake up the relationship by doing things differently. After being together so long, too many men and women tend to sway and that's when you're in trouble. That's when most women find themselves staying in a relationship when they want to go. So I say to all women, look deep inside your relationship, ask yourself why you're staying. Are you truly happy where you are? Did you build a foundation within your relationship where there is trust? Do you make time to laugh? Does your partner share the household responsibilities? Are you both pulling your weight and listening to each other? Or are there other reasons you're staying, such as financial responsibilities or you feel that you've invested too many years and don't want to start over? These are important questions you alone can answer. If you're being abused physically or mentally, get out—find a safe haven and tell someone. Don't put it off for another day; there is light at the end of the tunnel. I promise, any life is better than staying in an abusive relationship. Don't continue to get used to that lifestyle. You deserve better. Look in the mirror, start to love what you see in that mirror, see yourself in a happy place, feel the joy of life, of being in love, and put yourself there mentally. Once you can do that, your life will begin to change for the better. Know that you deserve to be happy; it takes some hard work and painful moments, and you can get there if you choose the road to happiness. Nothing is ever going to be perfect; there are always going to be bumps in the road or large potholes that we hit along the way, that's part of the growing pains, but I promise you that it's all going to be worth it in the end. Make your choices wisely; what road you want to take is your choice. If you stay in a relationship when you really want to go, you're really not being true to yourself. You're missing out; the sun is not shining in your world, and it can't shine or even come out until you realize there's a better life waiting for you. Put away your raincoat, your tears. You don't need that umbrella; you just need to believe in yourself and where you want to be in life. Choose to be happy with or without a relationship; just don't stay if you really want to go.

WHY WOMEN STAY WHEN THEY WANT TO GO

It was a cold, brisk winter's night,

The moon was shining bright,

The stars covered the sky

As the women stood there,

Thinking of how to say goodbye.

Why Women Stay When They Want to Go

She wanted to go,

She could not stay,

Not even for another day,

The love was gone,

The gloves came on,

The fighting just wouldn't stop,

Tears began to flow

As she started to go,

Then suddenly fear set in,

She thought, Where do I begin?

How do I start over?

I don't want to be alone, getting older.

As the sun came up,

The woman dried her tears,

And retreated unhappy for the next ten years,

She decided to stay when she wanted to go,

Afraid of change,

Afraid of letting go.

ABOUT THE AUTHOR

One of the ten children, Jeannie Middleton was born and raised in New York City along with her identical twin sister and best friend Jayne. The family moved to Richmond Hill, Queens, when she was ten and their parents bought their first house. It was like moving into a mansion! She first graduated with a degree, and then with a degree in psychology.

Jeannie loves spending time with family and friends, enjoying backyard barbeques, and the simple things in life. But most of all, she enjoys helping solve everyone's problems and being there for anyone in need of a friend. She currently lives in Lindenhurst, Long Island, with her husband of thirty years. Together they have a son, three lovely grandchildren, eight cherished great-grandchildren, three German shepherds, and two cats.